The Altered Book
Scrapbook

DOMAIN
73 d
ANNÉE

The Altered Book Scrapbook

Susan Ure

Chapelle, Ltd., Inc.
P.O. Box 9252, Ogden, UT 84409
(801) 621-2777 • (801) 621-2788 Fax
e-mail: chapelle@chapelleltd.com
Web site: www.chapelleltd.com

Every effort has been made to ensure that all information in this book is accurate. However, due to differing conditions, tools, and individual skills, the publisher cannot be responsible for any injuries, losses, and/or other damages, which may result from the use of the information in this book.

This volume is meant to stimulate crafting ideas. If readers are unfamiliar with or not proficient in a skill necessary to attempt a project, we urge that they refer to an instructional book specifically addressing the required technique.

Library of Congress Cataloging-in-Publication Data
Ure, Susan.
  The altered book scrapbook / Susan Ure.
      p. cm.
  "A Sterling/Chapelle Book."
  Includes index.
  ISBN-13: 978-1-4027-1327-9
  ISBN-10: 1-4027-1327-4
  1. Altered books. 2. Scrapbooks. I. Title.
  TT896.3.U73 2006
  745.593--dc22
                                                    2005034083

10 9 8 7 6 5 4 3 2 1
Published by Sterling Publishing Co., Inc.
387 Park Avenue South, New York, NY 10016
©2006 by Susan Ure
Distributed in Canada by Sterling Publishing
c/o Canadian Manda Group, 165 Dufferin Street
Toronto, Ontario, Canada M6K 3H6
Distributed in the United Kingdom by GMC Distribution Services,
Castle Place, 166 High Street, Lewes, East Sussex, England BN7 1XU
Distributed in Australia by Capricorn Link (Australia) Pty. Ltd.
P.O. Box 704, Windsor, NSW 2756, Australia
Printed in China
All Rights Reserved

Sterling ISBN-13: 978-1-4027-1327-9
        ISBN-10: 1-4027-1327-4

For information about custom editions, special sales, premium, and corporate purchases, please contact Sterling Special Sales Department at 800-805-5489 or specialsales@sterlingpub.com

(Above) Page from Shani Richart's *The Wedding*, shown on pages 70-75. (Opposite) Pages from Lisa Cook's *Florence*, shown on pages 114-119.

*This book is dedicated to all who take pleasure
in making old things new.*

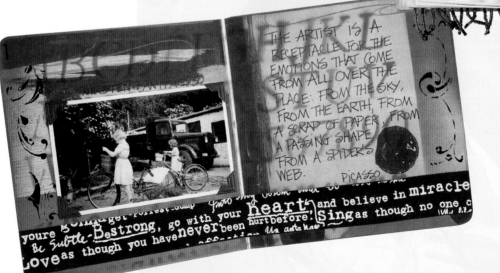

Table of Contents

LIFE IN THE OPEN
THE COMING OF SPRING
NORA PERRY

THERE'S something in the air
That's new and sweet and rare—
A scent of summer things,
A whir as if of wings.

There's something, too, that's new
In the color of the blue
That's in the morning sky,
Before the sun is high.

And though on plain and hill
'Tis winter, winter still,
There's something seems to say
That winter's had its day.

And all this changing tint,
This whispering stir and hint
Of bud and bloom and wing,
Is the coming of the spring.

"I foresee a book which . . . might disguise name, admit explain . . . might most completely change."
~ Tom Phillips

Introduction

Like most crafters and artists, I'm always excited to find new techniques, materials, and concepts for my projects. When I discovered altered books, I knew I had stumbled into a wide-open realm of creative possibility.

An altered book is one that has been transformed into an entirely different work of art. An early example is Tom Phillip's reworking of a Victorian novel, *A Humament*, published in the 1970s. The idea of combining altered books with scrapbooking has hit the crafting world only recently, but it has hit hard. Some are drawn to the freedom and flexibility of altered art, others love the accessibility of the raw materials, and still others can't resist the challenge of working with a preprinted text. No matter why you try altered book scrapbooking, I guarantee that if this is your first step into this creative form, it won't be your last.

As you'll see in the pages that follow, altered book scrapbooks can be as diverse as the people who create them. The ten artists whose work appears in this book share their unique interpretations of the themes Friends and Family, Discovery, Celebration, Inspiration, Places We Have Been, and Honoring the Past. In addition to inspiring layouts from more than a dozen altered book scrapbooks, they share their design insights and techniques to help ensure that when you begin your own projects, you'll have the information you need to express your unique style.

(Opposite) Pages from Susan Ure's *Prose and Poetry*, shown on pages 14-21.

9

Detail from Susan Ure's *Prose and Poetry*, shown on pages 14-21.

A Word About Materials

Most of the materials and tools you'll need to make an altered art scrapbook are standard scrapbooking supplies with a notable exception: as most books are not made of archival materials, it typically isn't worth the extra investment in archival-quality papers, embellishments, pigments, and adhesives you may usually use. For the historian in you, this may seem like bad news, but for the artist in you, it can be liberating. What can you do if you don't have to worry about longevity? What can you paint, glue, stamp, and otherwise attach to your pages? If you're like most of us who catch the altered art bug, you'll get in there and have a blast. Combine a copy of a treasured photo with a strip of newspaper. Sprinkle real flower petals across the page. Let yourself do things you've taught yourself not to do in your keepsake scrapbooks and see what new ideas you come up with.

Of course, if you are planning a particularly special project, it's possible to treat the pages of your book with an acid-neutralizing spray and to secure elements with longer-lasting methods such as brads, wire, or ribbon. A less expensive compromise is to back photos and other delicate elements with heavy, acid-free paper and cover them with an archival-quality sealant. While this won't make the page completely archival, it can at least slow down the aging process.

Getting Started

While you can add most anything to your altered book scrapbook, many of the projects featured in this book were made from basic materials and tools like these:

Materials

— Acrylic craft paints

— Copies of photographs

— Cord, ribbon, string, thread

— Double-sided tape

— Embellishments

— Fabric scraps

— Fasteners such as brads or eyelets

— Glues: craft glue stick, fine-tipped liquid glue, hot-glue gun and glue sticks, paste

— Hardcover book with spine and binding in good condition

— Papers of various weights, patterns, and textures

— Pencils, pens, and markers

— Wire

Tools

— Brushes for paint and glue

— Computer and printer

— Credit card for spreading glue

— Eyelet setter

— Hole punch

— Needles for sewing and making holes

— Ruler

— Scissors

— Stamps and inkpads

A Word About Techniques

Altered book scrapbooking is a fantastic way to develop your crafting skills. I think it's because each page in a book invites you to find different ways to express your creativity. The artists featured in the following pages will show you how they use paint, collage, stamping, stickers, needlework, and other techniques to turn books into personalized creations. We'll offer step-by-step instructions for finishing page edges, creating windows, layering, making pockets, sewing cloth covers, and more.

Finding Your Style

While some craft books focus on showing readers how to create specific layouts, this book aims to help you design projects that express your individual personality. As a designer, I often find that artists whose work is unlike my own can teach me amazing things that I might not learn from those I wish to emulate. That's one reason why this book features such a wide range of approaches. Whether you lean toward Victorian vintage, multicultural contemporary, or points beyond, I believe the projects here will get you thinking in new directions. Keep in mind that the trick to translating inspiration into unique creations lies in paying attention not just to the details of a project, but also to the general design principles an artist has followed. If you consider how a project uses color, texture, placement, and techniques from page to page, you'll be well on your way to making exciting discoveries of your own.

Detail from Susan Ure's *Prose and Poetry*, shown on pages 14-21.

(Above) A page from *Prose & Poetry* (Opposite, clockwise) Details from *Special Lady*, *Prose & Poetry*, and *Frani's Cafe*.

"What greater thing is there for human souls, than to feel that they are joined for life...?"
~ *George Eliot*

Chapter 1

Friends & FAMILY

Scrapbookers everywhere know that ours is an art that honors important personal relationships. Our creations can even help us to understand loved ones better, as I discovered while making *Prose & Poetry*. We can also preserve cherished memories to share with future generations, as Madeline Arendt does in *Special Lady*. And, when we use altered book techniques, we can make each album as unique as the people we celebrate, as you'll see with Lisa Hoffman's tribute to a friend in *Frani's Café*.

(Opposite) To make the base book's cover appear an organic part of my design, I incorporated shades of green and kept the title visible.

(Below) A handwritten note from the subject of the scrapbook helps make her or him a strong presence on the page.

"It isn't that I breathe life into the art—it's that art breathes life into me." ~ Susan Ure

When my brilliant, creative grandmother gave me the textbook she had used in her classes for many years, I was disappointed to see how dull it was. I realized, however, that she didn't choose her curricula and that the book was, in fact, a compromise between the prose of life and the poetry of her soul. As I altered it, I asked, "What would this book be like if it reflected Grandma Jody?"

When selecting elements for a spread, consider the meaning attached to an image. To me, feathers, stars, and leaves are all symbols of the wild spirit of the imagination.

Embraceable You

REMEMBRANCE

I think of one purple poppy
in the midst of a wheat-field,
suaver than silk in the bolt,
with the smell of a serpent. All
the rest bristles with wheat
gilded and scythed in the sheaf.

More than once I have coiled my whole
length where the threshers have passed
with a wilderness . . . sole
suddenly bit in two, to . . . moonlight
while an odor of semen . . .
arose from the quivering . . .

Speaking of Character

My grandmother had a sparkling personality to go with her clever mind. To help express her playful side, I had some fun of my own, adding a glitter-coated embellishment to her bodice, a pink ribbon skirt, and a gleaming Eiffel Tower crown.

Copy an original marriage license for a unique scrapbook paper. Grandma Jody, whose given name was Stella Beatrice, was married in the grand state of Texas.

The edge is an important part of a page. Why not make it as distinctive as the spread itself? By embellishing page edges, you can enhance your layouts while giving the unopen book an intriguing, sculptural feel. Bits of ribbon, beads, or other elements that are visible when the book is closed pique the reader's curiosity and act as tabs to particular sections.

It can be a challenge to find a photo of your forebears cutting loose. When you find one, treat it like the gold it is. Get it preserved and use copies of it in your artwork.

Passages cut from the base book's text can be added back onto the altered page in places that suit your design.

To create a window for photographs, cut a rectangle several pages deep, and place photo on the uncut, bottom page. Tuck decorative paper around the edges of the window, paste the pages together, and add frames.

Weave a wispy embroidered collar over an envelope and under a leaf to emphasize the dimensionality of a page.

Costume jewelry pins add a bit of glamour. To prevent the tip of a pin from tearing your page, cover the end of a pin with plastic, wax, or rubber if the original cap is missing.

Featured Technique

Finished Page Edge

Thick page edges beg for embellishment. Try dressing up the edges of your altered book with rows of tiny pearls and iridescent seed beads:

Materials

— Clear seed beads

— Fabric

— Fine-tipped glue

— Hot glue gun and glue sticks

— Pre-strung miniature pearls

— Ruler

— Scissors

— Sewing needle

— Thread

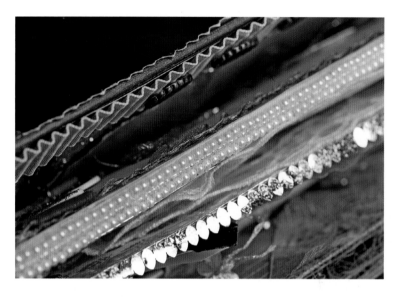

Instructions

1. Measure the length of the top, side, and bottom of the page. Add these three numbers to determine the total length of the page edge.

2. Cut one strip of fabric to the exact total length of the page edge.

3. Measure the depth of the page edge. Fold the sides of the fabric strip to be as wide as the page is deep. Use a baste stitch to hold it closed.

4. Adhere the fabric along the page edge, using fine-tipped glue.

5. Thread one strand of clear seed beads and cut two strands of miniature pearls to match the total length of the page edge.

6. Apply the beads and pearls to the fabric-covered edge, using the hot-glue gun and glue sticks.

If the base book has an image you want to use on a different page, cut it out and apply it as you would any other element.

Stamp a rectangle of cardstock with your own combination of images and tie on a Chinese coin to make an unusual embellishment.

PIONEERS! O PIONEERS!

Walt Whitman

For we cannot tarry here,
We must march, my darlings, we must bear the brunt of danger,
We the youthful sinewy races, all the rest on us depend,
Pioneers! O Pioneers!

togetherness /tu-'ge-[th]er-ness/ noun
1. association of mingling as friends
2. marked by an atmosphere of good fellowship

let's talk

Apply brown ink to the edges of a deckle-edged window and a paper sentiment to give them a charred look.

"What I love about altered book scrapbooking is that your 'album' is entirely unlike anyone else's. Anyone can go to the store and buy the same album. It's far less likely that anyone will use the same base book as you. Even if they do, there's next to no chance that they'll do the same things with it.

"For me, the process starts with the book and my subject. As I gather my materials, I get ideas about what I'm going to do, but I don't like to work from a fixed plan. I allow myself to get involved emotionally and let my thoughts carry me along. Being spontaneous leaves room for surprises, sudden insights, and strokes of inspiration. It keeps the act of creation an unfolding adventure."

~ Susan Ure

Special Lady

Madeline Arendt

Madeline Arendt's scrapbook honoring her mother is a great example of reaching a balance between continuity and variety within a book. While each page celebrates a different aspect of its subject's life and uses different layouts and elements, it also contains recurrent features such as roses to add to the sense of flow from one layout to the next.

> *"If you want to try a new craft, grab a book and get started. Don't worry about knowing all there is to know—you'll learn as you go along and have a great time, too."*
>
> *~ Madeline Arendt*

Many of the ribbons that appear throughout this scrapbook are tied off to form a tassel at the spine. This helps unify the overall design of the book by bringing materials from the interior pages to the exterior.

By selecting books with interesting features, you give yourself ample opportunity to achieve unusual effects.

Copies of photos can be artificially aged with a light application of sandpaper and brown dye-based ink along the edges.

Special Lady
Madeline Arendt

It is important to honor our beginnings, to remember that we matter and that we have a place in this world that no one else has.

child

\child\, n.; pl. children
A son or a daughter; a male or female descendant, in the first degree; the immediate progeny of human parents; — in law, legitimate offspring. Used also of animals and plants.

A harmonious design calls for an effective color scheme. Throughout *Special Lady*, Madeline relies heavily on a palette of cream, gold, and brown to unify new and old photographs and foster a classic, historical feel. This use of color helps make this altered book scrapbook a fine example of how to tell a story about a person through images and few words; the warmth of the colors helps the viewer sense the warmth of the subject's personality.

Print your own computer-generated sentiments or hand-letter your message on vellum.

Daughter

PARENTS
CLARA & JOHN SCHOUMACHER

home n.
1. A place where one lives; a residence. 2. The physical structure within which one lives, such as a house or apartment. 3. A dwelling place together with the family or social unit that occupies it; a household. 4. a. An environment offering security and happiness. b. A valued place regarded as a refuge or place of origin. 5. The place, such as a country or town, where one was born or has lived for a long period.

pa
1. O
nurtu
mothe
organ
offspr
paren
origin

Photocopy a length of lace or cut out a border from a piece of scrapbook paper for a two-dimensional embellishment.

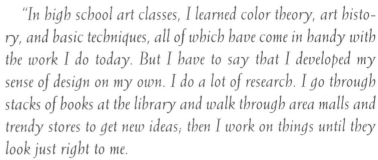

"In high school art classes, I learned color theory, art history, and basic techniques, all of which have come in handy with the work I do today. But I have to say that I developed my sense of design on my own. I do a lot of research. I go through stacks of books at the library and walk through area malls and trendy stores to get new ideas; then I work on things until they look just right to me.

"I like altered books because I love making something old current. Yet I also like to have a purpose for my projects. If I create a display piece for someone, I aim to make it something that will have personal meaning for them. I work with various media; right now, my top three are probably paper, fabric, and fiber embellishments—but that list could change tomorrow!"

~ Madeline Arendt

If your design calls for minimal journaling but you need to say more, write a message on a card. Glue together the bottom and top edges of two pages, leaving the side open to create a pocket for your card.

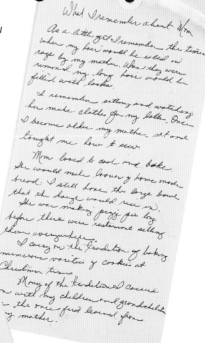

To give photos more presence on a page, mount them on coordinating papers and let the borders show.

DOLORES
MAY 26, 1922

IRENE
NOVEMBER 7, 1924

laughter
n 1: the sound of laughing [syn: laugh] —
activity of laughing: the manifestation o...
or mirth of scorn: "he enjoyed the laugh...
the crowd"

sib·ling
n. One of two or more individuals having one or both parents in common; a brother or sister.

Sisters share that unique & special relationship that combines friend and supportive and that is at the same time who shares her life with a sister is blessed.

Clear self-stick photo corners are an unobtrusive way to hold photos to a page.

Married November 5, 1938
to
George Palicki

Com·pan·ion

n. 1. one that accompanies another : one that keeps company with another. 2 a : one that is closely connected with something similar b : one employed to live with and serve another.

Another way to bring dimensionality to your scrapbook without adding too much weight or thickness is to combine photocopies or cut-out images with flatter elements such as buttons.

If you're aiming for a flat scrapbook, yet want to use three-dimensional embellishments, position them so that they don't touch when the book is closed.

To make this page stand out from the others, Madeline used ivory rickrack rather than gold paint to enhance the border.

29

Golden Years

love *n.*
1. A deep, tender, ineffable feeling of affection and solicitude toward a person, such as that arising from kinship, recognition of attractive qualities, or a sense of underlying oneness. 2. A feeling of intense desire and attraction toward a person with whom one is disposed to make a pair; the emotion of romance.

All the LOVE we come to know in life springs from the love we knew as children.

64

A paper doily mounted to the center of a page pulls together a layout featuring multiple photographs. Madeline recommends covering a paper doily with a coat of sealant after adhering it to the book.

All the
LOVE
we come to know in life
springs from the love
we knew as
children.

Featured Technique

Two-sided Window

The pattern of the doily adds subtle texture and dimension to a vellum sentiment on one page, while achieving an entirely different effect on the next.

Materials

— Children's board book with die-cut pages

— Clear-drying glue

— Crocheted doily, slightly larger than window

— Fringe/eyelash yarn

— Plastic heart mold

— Ribbon

— Ruler

— Scissors

— Small cloth roses

— Vellum sentiment

Instructions

1. Cut vellum to fit the die-cut window, with ¼" extra on every side.

2. Apply a thin border of glue around the back of the die-cut window. Place vellum sentiment face down on the glue, ensuring that it can be read from the front.

3. Loop and glue yarn to center of doily. Adhere the doily to the back of the die-cut window so that it covers the vellum. Use extra glue if necessary.

4. Tie ribbon and roses to the corner of the heart mold. Glue the embellished mold to the center of the doily.

love n.
1. A deep, tender, ineffable feeling of affection and solicitude toward a person, such as that arising from kinship, recognition of attractive qualities, or a sense of underlying oneness. 2. A feeling of intense desire and attraction toward a person with whom one is disposed to make a pair; the emotion of romance.

The title of the previous page peers through the window, connecting Marcelle's marriage to George with the love of their offspring.

Decorative corner punches are an easy way to give photos a flourish.

Golden Years

Mother

a shoulder to cry on
a smile to count on
a love to live on

grandmother
\Grand"moth"er\.
n. The mother of one's father or mother.

All the
LOVE
we come to know in life
springs from the love
we knew as
children.

great grandmother

patience
\Pa'tience\. n.

1. The state or quality of being patient; the power of suffering with fortitude; uncomplaining endurance of evils or wrongs, as toil, pain, poverty, insult, oppression, calamity, etc.

By including the definition of patience, this layout acknowledges the strength it takes to be the kind of mother that children, grandchildren, and great-grandchildren rely on.

Rather than allowing your scrapbook to simply trail off, consider ways you can bring it to a satisfying conclusion. One method is to create a layout that summarizes the rest of the scrapbook. This is easier to do if you have developed a clear theme from page to page. After presenting layouts that celebrate the subject's importance to her family as a daughter, sister, wife, and mother, Madeline ends with photos of Marcelle's grandchildren, reinforcing the message that the Special Lady is in the center of many people's lives.

As the only color photograph in the layout, the solo image of Marcelle in the upper right corner stands out. An ivory ribbon frame further highlights her importance.

(Opposite) To create this cover, Lisa began with a layer of gesso, then she added layers of paint, loading her brush with multiple hues for a more "painterly" effect. She stamped the title, using permanent dye-based ink. To finish, she outlined the flower in oil pastels and sprayed the entire cover with a non-yellowing spray fixative.

In *Frani's Café*, Lisa Hoffman celebrates a friend whose warmth, generosity, and fabulous cooking have nourished their friendship for many years. Throughout the scrapbook, Lisa uses layers of paint to produce dynamic backgrounds and a visual murmur that mimics the comfortable hum of activity at Frani's place. Though Lisa hoped her friend would fill the book with recipes and keep it in the kitchen "where it would get covered with spaghetti sauce," Frani insists on treating it like a work of art, displaying it in a place of honor on the living-room table.

Throughout this scrapbook, layers of paint are used to produce dynamic backgrounds for Lisa's layouts. For the inside cover, blue paint atop a layer of gesso was repeatedly stamped with a large flower motif.

The first divider in this recipe binder was a great place to announce the spirit of adventure with which Frani approaches cooking and life. By placing these images so close together, Lisa hints that, for Frani, the heart just might be a compass.

Rough lines for borders, created with black permanent marker and electrical tape, enhance the impression of spontaneous creativity that seems such a part of Frani's life.

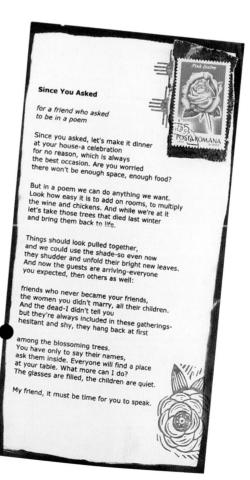

"Some people describe my style as 'folk art' or 'outsider art,' but I'm not particularly concerned about labels. I do the best work I can and try to keep a sense of humor. The minute you take your work too seriously, you create a chasm between yourself and your audience. After all, who wants art made by someone with a rockstar ego?

"Altered art is great because people with different skills and interests do it, resulting in an exciting variety of work. For me, altered book scrapbooking was a logical development from personal journaling. I've long kept written and visual journals and was strongly influenced by the book The Journey is the Destination: The Journals of Dan Eldon. It's amazing what we can do when we commit to honoring both the world around us and the worlds we hold inside."
~ Lisa Hoffman

On one side of the card, a collage; on the other, an original poem.

If you enjoy writing, why not include a poem dedicated to the subject of your scrapbook?

Since You Asked

for a friend who asked
to be in a poem

Since you asked, let's make it dinner
at your house-a celebration
for no reason, which is always
the best occasion. Are you worried
there won't be enough space, enough food?

But in a poem we can do anything we want.
Look how easy it is to add on rooms, to multiply
the wine and chickens. And while we're at it
let's take those trees that died last winter
and bring them back to life.

Things should look pulled together,
and we could use the shade-so even now
they shudder and unfold their bright new leaves.
And now the guests are arriving-everyone
you expected, then others as well:

friends who never became your friends,
the women you didn't marry, all their children.
And the dead-I didn't tell you
but they're always included in these gatherings-
hesitant and shy, they hang back at first

among the blossoming trees.
You have only to say their names.
ask them inside. Everyone will find a place
at your table. What more can I do?
The glasses are filled, the children are quiet.

My friend, it must be time for you to speak.

she also understood that
where her street ended.
the rest of the world began.

To unify disparate elements, such as an image of the
Mona Lisa and a photo of Frani, give each a similar
halo of painted dots.

A very dark or very light image makes a great background for a painted detail such as this heart.

whats
on THE
Menu!

inspire

The rainbow runs through my eyes.

COOKiN UP THE → future

"*Free your imagination by making a sacrificial piece that no one will ever see. It's amazing how easy it is to lose your inhibitions when you stop trying to Make Art and simply let yourself have a good time.*"
~ *Lisa Hoffman*

It was a long time ago, but the Recipe was MAGic... it was a mix of all of the right people at just the right time. Some things have gone so well for all of us, a few things NEVER should have happened, but through it ALL we have EaCh OtHeR ♡♡♡

100% authentic

Ah! There's nothing like staying home for real comfort.
- Jane Austen

OuR tRibe

SCAttereD

Keep in mind the purpose of your book when designing a layout. Because *Frani's Café* is meant to hold pages of recipes between each altered divider, Lisa didn't need to worry about fashioning adjacent dividers as a single spread. She uses this creative freedom to the fullest, allowing her own wild style and photos of the same people to unify the work. In a sense, Lisa faces—and answers—the same design question seen in *Special Lady*, that of balancing theme and variation from page to page.

Lisa uses a conversational tone in some of the textual elements to give the viewers a sense that they're part of the fun.

Featured Technique

Layering

Through layering, one can combine simple two-dimensional elements like paint, photos, and stamping into a composition of delightful complexity.

Materials

— Acrylic paints; aqua, lilac, orange, yellow

— Brushes for paint and sealant

— Clear acrylic sealant

— Cut-out images from magazine and newspaper

— Gesso

— Inks: reddish brown, red

— Oil crayons: blue, green, purple

— Photographs

— Rubber stamps: flower border, travel design, sentiments

Instructions

1. Apply a layer of gesso to the page.

2. Paint the page orange, allowing a little gesso to show through in a few places.

3. Paint an aqua square. Dab three splotches of yellow paint along the left border.

4. Stamp a flower border and travel-oriented designs in reddish-brown ink. Stamp sentiments such as "Yummy" and "All Time Fave" in red ink.

5. Glue images from a newspaper, photographs, and a magazine onto the page.

6. Create borders around key elements, using paint and oil crayons. Restamp any designs as needed.

7. Brush a coat of sealant over the photograph.

As every thread of gold is valuable,
so is every minute of time - mason

INnOCenT

Speak French when you
can't think of the English
for a thing — turn out
your toes as you walk —
and remember who you are.
— Lewis Carroll

The wrapper from a bar of soap can make an
excellent background.

Stamp the frame of an old photo slide to create an unusual embellishment.

Black electrical tape is decorative as well as functional when your style is as contemporary as Lisa's.

growth

Babies know when they are loved.
P. H. HANES KNITTING CO.

alert and happy, while others are
and solemn. But each baby is lov-
his own way. You may think of
quiet ones as "good babies." And
are good; but so are the active
Babies and small children who
or dash about from one thing to
and are "always into some-
are just following their natura

babies grow, they all need to e
limb, and handle objects to lea
the things that interest them.

anticip

"Trust yourself. You know more than you think you do."
~ Benjamin Spock

(Above) Pages from *The Mommy Journey*. (Opposite) Details of leaf and sunburst tag from *Nature Journeys*; detail pocket and tag from *The Mommy Journey*.

Chapter 2

DISCOVERY

When your scrapbook focuses on a single person, your theme comes ready-made. But there are other ways to unify the various spreads you wish to create, such as choosing a particular experience or environment your subjects share. For instance, in *The Mommy Journey*, Shani Richart marks the transition into motherhood with photos and journaling that depict the beginning of her new baby's life. In *Nature Journeys*, I brought together images of various family members enjoying the great outdoors.

When Shani Richart found an old Home Economics book in a thrift store, she knew it was perfect for a scrapbook on her transition into motherhood. The textbook's wholesome messages about keeping a home are so charming that Shani left many of the pages untouched, allowing viewers to read lessons on nutrition, cooking, and sewing. Shani's colorful layouts and exuberant text burst from the pages to create a message of love that she can pass on to her children.

Featured Technique

Door Cover with Inset

An interactive feature such as a door can make your book's cover more enticing. A transparency and embellished flyleaf pull in the viewer even deeper.

Materials

— 2 Brass hinges

— 8 Brass screws and washers

— Craft knife

— Drill and ⅛" bit

— Hardcover book

— Paint

— Paintbrush

— Small screwdriver

Take the viewer on a journey with a door that opens onto not one but two images. Here, a flap in the cover opens onto a transparency, behind which we see a picture of another door leading to rich green fields.

Instructions

1. Paint the cover of the book. Allow it to dry thoroughly.

2. Cut out all sides of a rectangle in the center of the cover, using your craft knife. Paint the cut edges of the newly created frame and the loose piece that will become the door.

3. Use a hinge as a template to mark the location for screws on the frame and door. Drill small holes and screw the hinges into place. Secure the back of each screw with a washer.

A wash of brown ink stamped with a crackle pattern transforms a page from the base book into a textured background. To make new copies of family photos resemble timeworn originals, bend them, drawn on them, and wash them with brown ink.

embrace your heritage

Vintage

LETTERS

Lovely

go on
and do
as good as you look

Ethan
those women
went before us
& Now
I have
you!

> "Let the photos that you use inspire the rest of your art. By making them the starting point for your designs, you will be better able to tell their stories."
>
> ~ Shani Richart

1. Always have Kleenex on hand
2. Naps may not come naturally
3. When you least expect it they WILL delight yo...

SECRETS

Of being a Mom:

GETTING THERE
IS ALL THE FUN.

Sometimes, a simple graphic layout is the best way to present a photograph. Bronze paint brushed across the crumpled green paper background adds depth to this understated design.

The Mommy Journey

Shani Richart

"Making art helps me recharge. I have a toddler and a newborn, so finding time to be creative is as important as ever to me. Fortunately, as a photographer I can work in moments for art here and there by taking snapshots. When I have time to myself, I use the photos in projects such as altered book scrapbooks.

"For me, altered book scrapbooking is very freeing. Oddly enough, starting with something besides a blank page makes it easier to forget the 'rules.' I frequently combine photography, stamping, drawing, journaling, and collage in my altered books. My first altered book was actually an official school textbook that I wrote in as a kid. I'd leave a message and direct the reader to another page, then another. Now my work is a bit more involved, but the spirit of adventure is the same."

~ Shani Richart

Shani chose to let parts of the base book show through by folding back the corners and gluing them to the back of the page. A plastic eyelet holds the corner in place and a round paperclip embellished with ruby-colored beads holds a humorous message to the page.

A light application of purple paint to the edges of the text and the photograph ties these elements together.

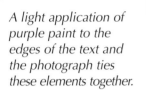

Try fabric paint for flexible, translucent backgrounds. A coat of pearl paint adds an intriguing sheen.

For a decorative border that also secures a section of pages, punch tiny holes into the edge of the pages and sew them together with beaded wire.

An alternative way to include photos and mementos in your scrapbook is to tuck them into pocket pages. Simply tear consecutive pages at staggered intervals and glue only the top and bottom edges to create pockets. If you wish to highlight the border of each pocket, paint and stamp each page before you tear.

We loved adding your footprint to our family!

We took you to NagsHead in July 04. The Richards

you loved the beach so that makes us

When planning your layout, remember that high-profile embellishments may become damaged when the scrapbook is closed. To protect delicate elements such as these shells, cut a rectangular hole into several pages of the base book, adhere the pages to a sturdy uncut page, and place the embellishments in the nook.

Sometimes the simplest layouts can be the most challenging to do well. After all, with minimal elements on the page, your technical skills are front and center. To increase the odds of getting the look you want, take your time. Plan carefully and assemble the tools you need to do the job right. For instance, if your design calls for a perfect straight edge, consider using a paper trimmer to get the clean lines you want.

When I saw Maryjo Koch's nature book *Bird Egg Feather Nest,* my theme for a new family scrapbook clicked into place: I wanted to show my loved ones playing outdoors, in the simple pursuit of being themselves. As a base, Koch's book provided such beautiful illustrations and hand-lettered text that I was able to incorporate the original pages into many of my layouts. *Nature Journeys* is the altered book scrapbook that resulted.

(Opposite) Handmade paper gives the cover of this altered book a soft, luxurious feel and miniature glass squares add a touch of glamour. A yellow pansy peers through a hand-cut window. To dry a pansy without flattening it, try silica sand, which is available at craft stores.

Finish off the inside covers for a more polished scrapbook. This can be as simple as adhering plain paper in place or as involved making them part of a layout. This design takes the middle route—minimal embellishment with eyelash yarn, ribbon, and handmade labels.

Flexible plastic leaves on wire look delicate, yet are durable enough to act as decorative page tabs.

"What is it?" he asked very respectfully. "that has given you such beautiful voices? Is there any special food you eat, or is it some divine nectar that makes you sing so wonderfully?"

"How very, very anxious you are about me," she said.

Passages and illustrations from a classic such as Aesop's Fables *can become a charming motif throughout a scrapbook.*

A miniature glue dot holds a fossil-leaf wing to a photograph of my favorite garden fairy, Forrest.

Sew heavy charms into place for a longer-lasting scrapbook. An easy method is to pierce holes in the photo, adhere it to the page, then stitch the charm into place.

60

To carry the effect of the tree's ridges into my background, I made 1"-deep folds in vellum paper and glued them in place with white glue. A paperclip at the top and bottom of each fold helps it dry securely.

Moss and tree bark are a natural choice for embellishing a page like this—and they may be as close as your own backyard.

b
[baby]

fresh (fresh) 1. recently made, grown 2. not spoiled 3. not tired, lively 4. new, recent

JeSaia

"*Scrapbooking makes me more confident out in the world because it helps me clarify who I am and what I value. What subjects do I choose? How do I present them? My creations show me what I truly value.*"   *~ author*

Nature belongs to
the eyes that see it.

—Ralph Waldo Emerson

chad

Discover
to be the first to find

JES & Forrest

A Butterfly once fell in love

Forrest

Maryjo Koch's illustrations peer through patches of natural fiber paper. It's the interplay between an artist's design and the features of a base book that makes the altered book approach so different from regular scrapbooking.

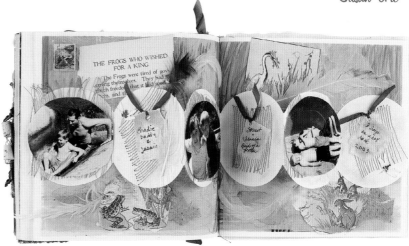

Featured Technique

Banner

Banners are a great way to work multiple images into a layout while adding three-dimensional interest. You can make this style of banner fit between the edges of any spread by adjusting the size of the circles in the "chain."

Materials

— 3 Mounted labels

— 3 Mounted photographs

— Compass

— Glue stick

— Pencil

— Ruler

— Scissors

— Sturdy paper

Instructions

1. Measure the length between the edges of your layout. Divide it by eight to determine the diameter of your circles.

2. Use the compass to draw eight circles on the paper, making sure that they are in a straight line and that their sides touch. Cut out the circles, taking care to keep the parts that touch intact.

3. Glue a mounted photograph or label to every circle in the chain except for the first and last.

4. Fanfold the circles.

5. Use the glue stick to adhere the first circle to the back of the left page and the second circle to the front of the left page.

6. Use the glue stick to adhere the seventh circle to the front of the right page and the eighth circle to the back of the right page.

Some layouts simply demand as much stuff as you can possibly fit onto a page. The theme of this layout is the sublime silliness of three kids having a great time together. In my mind, it called for lots of trinkets as small as the things that spark a fit of the giggles.

(Above) Pages from *Tis the Season*. (Opposite) Details of heart and couple from *The Wedding*; detail of snowflake from *Tis the Season*.

"If any one faculty of our nature may be called more wonderful than the rest, I do think it is memory."
~ Jane Austen

Chapter 3

CELEBRATION

All scrapbooks are a form of celebration, and the altered book scrapbook is no exception. This chapter shows different ways to create albums that make people smile. For instance, Shani Richart celebrates a relationship in the charming mini-scrapbook *The Wedding*, while Madeline Arendt captures holiday cheer in *'Tis the Season*. Both books are highly interactive, using features such as pockets and doors to draw readers into the fun.

(Opposite) Chalk, diamond dust, and letters in stamped gold ink enhance the embossed design on the base booklet. A circular paperclip at the top completes the composition.

Shani Richart wanted a wedding scrapbook she could carry with her. A lightweight booklet of paper samples from her local print shop proved perfect with images, text, and pockets that fit Shani's design concept nicely. Using techniques such as transfers and inking, Shani enriched the delicate pages into a confection of a book she can pull from her purse whenever she's in the mood for something sweet.

The romance continues! An insert celebrates the couple's life together with a series of anniversary photos. Black cardstock is fanfolded to tuck neatly inside the back cover pocket.

Diverse textures are another way to make an interactive book more fun. Here, soft strands of yarn invite the reader to tug out an envelope holding a love note, and a glossy tag contrasts nicely with the matte finish of a background.

With interactive elements, artists gain more room to express their ideas and readers have more nooks and crannies to explore. At first glance, this page seems simple with its preprinted image of a pear and text. Yet the flap reveals a wedding cake—part of a photo on a card you can pull out of the pocket.

72

Featured Technique

Packing Tape Transfer

Packing tape transfers are a simple way to achieve a subtle image. If you wish to use this technique with your own images, copy them on a commercial, toner-based printer rather than an inkjet printer.

Materials

— Clear-drying glue (optional)

— Image cut from a glossy magazine

— Packing tape

— Paper

— Water

Instructions

1. Place a strip of packing tape over the image.

2. Soak the packing tape and image in water for 5 minutes.

3. Roll the paper off of the packing tape, leaving ink from the image on the tape.

4. Press the tape onto the paper. Use glue to adhere it in place if the tape has lost its stickiness.

On one side of a tag, a romantic portrait of the couple. On the other side, a message reads: "Our wedding day on the beach was more beautiful than I ever imagined." Requiring readers to flip tags is yet another way to create a sensation-oriented experience.

Time to say "I love you?"
Take a word from Wordsworth.

married barefoot and on the beach.

On, be wise, Thou! instructed that true knowledge leads to love.
William Wordsworth

—little unremembered acts of kindness and love are the best parts of a person's life.
William Wordsworth

The Bahamas

Freeport
Eleuthera
Nassau
Cable
Beach
Exuma   Long Island
ks & Caicos

jasmine
A central ingredient in Hindu love potions for
centuries. Once believed to be a fast-acting aphrodisiac
for both sexes. Now known to be poisonous.

ginger
Passion and potency are its trademarks.
Promotes confidence and assertiveness.

patchouli
Has been used to increase sexual energy. An exotic
scent frequently found in incenses for the bedroom.

orange
Has adorned bridal wreaths for centuries to
increase the arousal of the groom. Also used by
prostitutes in Spain for its seductive powers.

juniper
Once believed to restore waning passions.
Also thought to remove negativity brought
from past relationships.

sage
Thought to relax muscles, lower inhibitions,
and increase blood flow throughout the body.

beware
the long love letter.

*Selecting a base book that has
elements that are visually appealing
and appropriate to your theme enables
you to play with the meeting point
between the inherited work and your
invention, as Shani does here.*

love letters
in the
sand

~ on a day like today
we passed the time
away

writing love letters
in the
sand...

"I love to learn from others. When I learn a new technique, I like to use it right away and develop my own variations of it."
~ Shani Richart

Love Notes

HOTEL
JUN 5 1901
MONIKER

passion?

be the food of
love, play on!" – Shakespeare

night and day
Cole Porter

Chad & Shani

Carmichael, Mitchell Parish

bolero
Maurice Ravel

For years, Madeline brought out a special family scrapbook during the holidays for family and guests to enjoy. When the scrapbook was lost in a shipping mishap, she mourned its loss. To keep this valuable part of her family tradition alive, she created a new holiday scrapbook by altering a children's lift-the-flap board book with images and sentiments that celebrate the meaning of family and Christmas.

When creating a scrapbook that you want family and visitors to flip through each year, be sure to design a durable cover. The baby mittens, ribbons, and bells that decorate the spine of this book will withstand both life in storage and plenty of handling, even by the youngest members of your tribe.

To prepare the base page, Madeline sanded the surface and sprayed it with gesso, applying multiple layers for thorough coverage.

The flaps bring an interactive feature to the book that makes this scrapbook even more fun to share with children during the holidays.

Featured Technique

Pocket Presents

These easy-to-make pockets are great for spreads celebrating birthdays, anniversaries, and other gift-giving occasions. A woodsy combination of dark reds and forest greens make for a cozy holiday layout while touches of scarlet and ivory keep the mood cheerful.

Materials

— Clear photo corners

— Eyelet setter and eyelet

— Glue stick

— Heavy scrapbook paper

— Lightweight cardboard

— Pencil

— Mounted photograph, 4" square

— Ribbon

— Ruler

— Scissors

— White craft glue

Instructions

1. Measure and cut two 4½" x 5" pieces of cardboard. Set the first piece aside.

2. Measure, mark, and cut a 1/2" margin around three sides of the second piece of cardboard to form a squared-off "U" shape. Use craft glue to adhere the U shape to the decorated page, open end up.

3. Cover the first piece of cardboard with scrapbook paper, using the glue stick. Tuck the scrapbook paper around the edges for complete coverage.

4. Tie ribbon around the center of the decorated cardboard. Secure to the back of the cardboard with craft glue.

5. Measure and cut a 1" x 5" strip of cardboard to make a lid for the present. Repeat Steps 3 and 4 to add scrapbook paper and ribbon.

6. Adhere the cardboard strip to the top of present. Adhere the present to the U-shaped base on the page.

7. Tuck a mounted photo into the hollow of the present.

By leaving some windows empty, Madeline has room for future additions to this family scrapbook.

For a layout with a touch of holiday sound, try tying tiny jingle bells to the flaps.

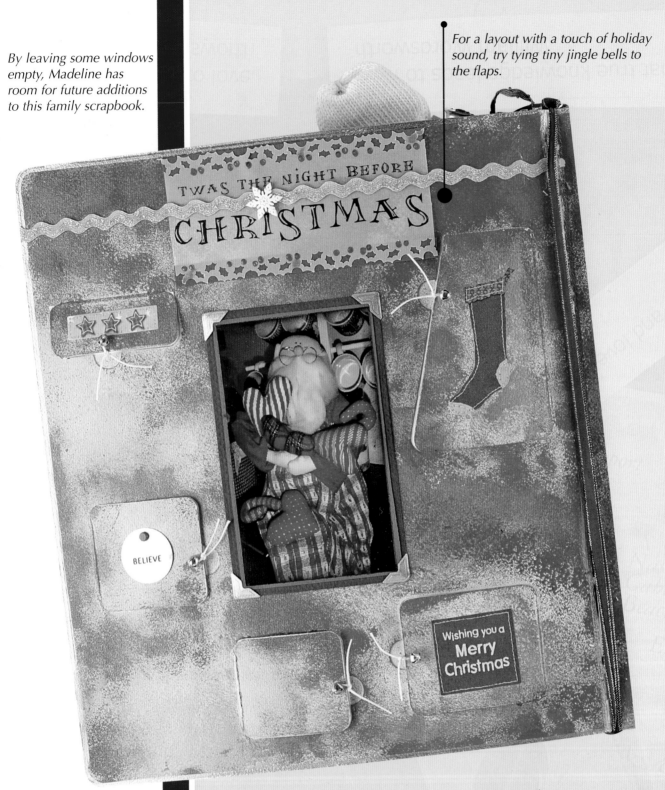

TWAS THE NIGHT BEFORE CHRISTMAS

BELIEVE

Wishing you a **Merry Christmas**

"What's most important to me is that I truly love what I do and hope to help others experience the joy of creating handmade pieces of art." ~ *Madeline Arendt*

80

Tis the Season

Madeline Arendt

What represents family togetherness? For Madeline's family, gathering around the holiday tree is just the beginning. Under each flap of this book is a reminder of a sentiment or a shared experience to help family members feel closer to each other during the holidays.

Red and green rickrack runs along the crease of the pages and is tied off as part of the embellishment for the front cover.

Gold safety pins are a homey way to apply tags to white rickrack. Apply rickrack with fine-tipped fabric glue.

JEAN 1935

(Above) Pages from *Pat & Maude & Mae*. (Opposite) Details of baby and pin from *Defining My Blessings*; detail of black flourish design from *Pat & Maude, & Mae*.

"What was art but a mould in which to imprison for a moment the shining elusive element which is life itself . . . too strong to stop, too sweet to lose."
~ *Willa Cather*

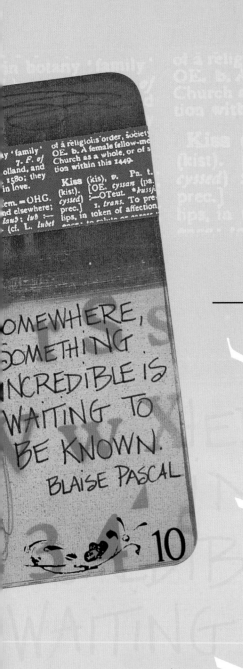

SOMEWHERE, SOMETHING INCREDIBLE IS WAITING TO BE KNOWN.
BLAISE PASCAL

10

Chapter 4

INSPIRATION

What moves you to embrace your better nature? How can you share that inspiration with others? Through an altered book scrapbook, of course. In *Pat & Maude & Mae*, Sarah Fishburn combines Depression-era photos with quotations for a powerful statement about life viewed with hopeful eyes. Andrea Vetten-Marley takes a different approach, turning a dictionary into *Defining Blessings of My Life*. The two scrapbooks differ from each other thematically and technically, yet both present images and ideas that readers may find uplifting.

AN ILLUSTRATED ALBUM OF QUOTES

PAT + MAUDE + MAE

Pat & Maude & Mae

Sarah Fishburn

(Opposite) As with several of the photographs in this scrapbook, Sarah rescued this image from a stack destined for a friend's trash-bin. All anyone knows of these young women are the names penciled on the back—Pat, Maude, and Mae.

Sarah Fishburn's scrapbook is so pretty that it may be easy to overlook its visual and conceptual depth. The astute use of color and placement shows that you don't need loads of elements to make lovely pages. By selecting photographs of young people in the 1930s and quotations from the likes of Einstein and Pascal, Sarah created a book that reminds us that beauty, strength, and joy can be found even in the darkest times.

Selecting a scrapbook paper with features such as dark circles and stripes reduces the need for embellishments, helping keep pages flat. By using original photos rather than copies, you can retain the authentic feel you might otherwise achieve with higher-profile details.

A whisper-thin border of copper paint adds warmth to each page and helps unify the different layouts.

Growing up in the Thirties didn't stop Sarah's father from having a great time and entertaining his family with his sense of humor.

4

ALL GROWN-UPS WERE
ONCE CHILDREN,
THOUGH FEW OF THEM
REMEMBER IT.

ANTOINE DE
SAINT EXUPER

3

BILLY

Post
Toasties
The Better Corn Flakes

iF YOU KNOW YOU'RE
GOING TO LOOK BACK
ON TODAY AND LAUGH,

s because what youre going ge
an hear you. Love as though

YOU MIGHT AS WELL
START LAUGHING
NOW.

ANONYMOUS

Cloth ribbon or gaffer tape is another way to add texture without overbuilding a page.

Featured Technique

Two-dimensional Texture

For a flat profile, try layering colors and elements on your background paper rather than building it up with embellishments. To improve the longevity of a photograph mounted to a non-archival background, apply a coat of acid-free acrylic sealer to the base page before you add the photograph.

Materials

— Alphabet stencils

— Board book

— Copper rub-on

— Credit card

— Newspaper

— Paste

— Pencil

— Photo corners

— Photograph

— Pink spray paint

— Scrapbook paper

— Scissors

— Wide brush for paste

Pat & Maude & Mae

Sarah Fishburn

Instructions

1. Spread out your scrapbook paper on newspaper in a well-ventilated area. Place alphabet stencils on the paper and spray with pink paint. For a soft look, do not tape down the stencils. Allow paper to dry thoroughly.

2. Cut painted scrapbook paper into the correct size and shape to fit the page. Spread paste across the back, using a credit card to ensure even distribution if necessary.

3. Position the paper over the base page. Align one edge carefully and roll the rest of the paper into place, smoothing it as you go. Set a heavy book or other weight on top of it until it dries.

4. Rub on a light copper border around the page.

5. Add photograph, penciled quotation, and gaffer tape.

"It doesn't matter whether you're a novice or an expert. It's important to keep in mind that someday somebody younger than you will come along and be inspired by what you've done."

~ Sarah Fishburn

Is anything more inspiring than the smile on a child's face? By limiting herself to minimal sentiments and one quotation per spread, Sarah allows the photos to speak for themselves.

The range of human experience includes hardships, such as those faced by children during the Great Depression of the 1930s. By choosing photographs from this era, Sarah created a scrapbook that can inspire readers to overcome their challenges.

THE DIFFICULT I CAN DO TODAY. THE IMPOSSIBLE WILL TAKE A LITTLE LONGER

BILL

JEAN + NANCY + JOAN

FRIENDSHIP IS BORN THE MOMENT WHEN ONE PERSON SAYS TO ANOTHER, "WHAT?! YOU TOO! I THOUGHT I WAS THE ONLY ONE" C.S. LEWIS

ROBERT + MARION + FRANK + GERTRUDE

"Though I took art classes in college, I really learned the value of art from my mom. She always had us make funky ornaments at Christmastime and was always up to something creative and clever, despite her full-time job as a nurse. I feel that everyone should have art in their lives, no matter what they do for a living. How do you remember the good things from hard times? How do you manage to make things beautiful for yourself? To me, the answer is art.

"Combining altered books and scrapbooking comes naturally to me since I've always liked interesting combinations. I love the personal challenge of putting my mark on something that already exists. Not only are you recycling, you're also collaborating with a person who is probably long gone. How swell is that?"
~ Sarah Fishburn

Five young women make light with a mock funeral on the beach. "This is exactly something my own daughters would do, only the photo was taken seventy years ago." Sarah says, "It just had to be in the album."

COMPILED AND ILLUSTRATED

BY SARAH FISHBURN

Defining Blessings of My Life

Andrea Vetten-Marley

While the old adage tells us to "count our blessings," Andrea Vetten-Marley defines hers instead. Starting with an old hardcover dictionary, she created pages to celebrate the various people she treasures. While part of the fun of altered book art is that you can make your pages whatever you want them to be, it's particularly interesting to see how Andrea uses the text of her base book in her layouts.

(Opposite) To create this cover, Andrea machine-stitched pieces of patterned paper together and added Scrabble letters, rub-ons, and three-dimensional letters to support the dictionary theme and provide visual interest.

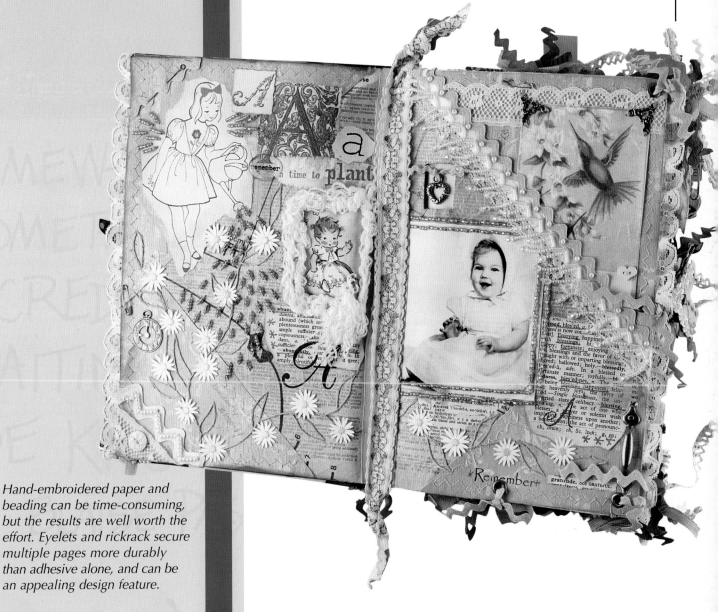

Hand-embroidered paper and beading can be time-consuming, but the results are well worth the effort. Eyelets and rickrack secure multiple pages more durably than adhesive alone, and can be an appealing design feature.

For a more masculine layout that is equally appropriate for pictures of a baby, a child, and a young man, try a simple color scheme and graphic layout.

To attach these buttons, Andrea sewed through both the floral paper she had glued in place and five pages of the base book. She then placed eyelets through an additional five pages of the base book and secured them with rickrack ties. The result is that the thread holding the buttons is hidden, and the reader can easily flip to the next layout.

Defining Blessings in My Life

Andrea Vetten-Marley

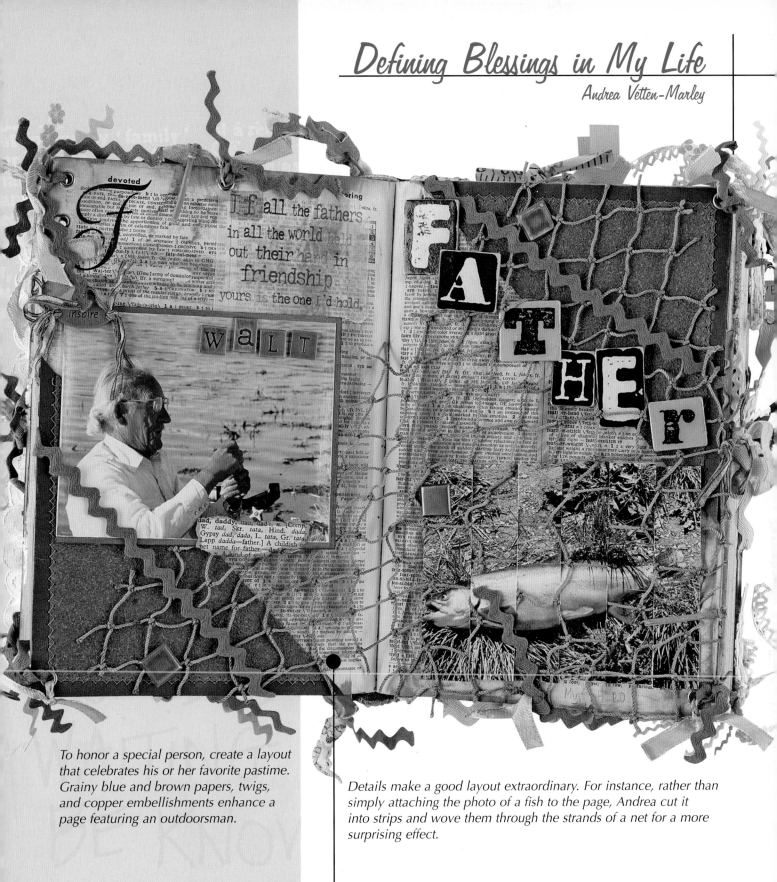

To honor a special person, create a layout that celebrates his or her favorite pastime. Grainy blue and brown papers, twigs, and copper embellishments enhance a page featuring an outdoorsman.

Details make a good layout extraordinary. For instance, rather than simply attaching the photo of a fish to the page, Andrea cut it into strips and wove them through the strands of a net for a more surprising effect.

The image of a rose window on the original dictionary page shows through just enough to become a subtle design element in this layout.

Enhance the effect of a design by using mu techniques to repeat the same motif on a s page. Here, whimsical flowers are embroid stamped, and glued to the page.

This rickrack picks up the hue of Gillian's shirt, unifying the overall layout with the photographs.

Girls just wanna have fun

Girl

S - M - L

50% Sugar
40% Spice
10% Nice

Gentle Cycle

Giggle

Defining Blessings of My Life

Andrea Vetten-Marley

"I love doing altered book scrapbooks because there's an added layer of history, texture, and dimension to a project. And even though you start with someone else's creation, altered art is very personal because every one of us would take the same starting point and work in a different direction based on our unique experiences and personalities.

"Needlecraft tends to be a big part of my work. When I was a child, my grandmothers taught me to sew, and when I became a mother, I sewed even more because I couldn't find exactly what I wanted. (I think this is how most designers are born— no one makes what they want, so they make it themselves.) I use a lot of memorabilia in my projects as well. I love collecting it, and so scrapbooking gives me an excuse to add to my collection."   ~ Andrea Vetten-Marley

A photo of three generations of mothers standing behind children says a great deal about the power of a mother's love.

Consider including images of locations where family gather, such as a photo of Grandma's house.

Costume jewelry such as this vintage pin makes ideal embellishments for altered book scrapbooks.

Featured Technique

Hand-stitched Pages

Repeating techniques such as sewing is another way to communicate that different sections of a scrapbook are all part of one composition. Andrea carried her sewing theme onto the cover itself, stitching papers together for a pretty, patchwork effect.

Materials

— Beads, if desired

— Embroidery needle

— Eyelet setter and eyelets

— Foam or cork

— Hole punch

— Sewing needle

— Spray adhesive

— Ribbon, rickrack, or string

— Thread

"If you get stuck, don't push it. Instead, move on to another project until you know what to do with the first one. Sometimes, I have a dozen layouts going at a time, so I have plenty to work on while individual projects have time to breathe."

~ Andrea Vetten-Marley

Defining Blessings of My Life
Andrea Vetten-Marley

Instructions

1. Adhere a few pages of the base book together, using spray adhesive.

2. Place foam or cork behind the pages. Use the embroidery needle to pierce holes along the line you intend to sew.

3. Sew through the holes, adding beads if desired.

4. Use spray adhesive to adhere a few more pages to the back of the sewed page.

5. Finish by punching holes along the edges of adhered pages and adding eyelets, following manufacturer's instructions on your eyelet setter. Tie ribbon, rickrack, or string through the eyelets.

STORMY

WEATH

weather (weth'ĕr), n. the state of
the atmosphere with respect to cold,
heat, wet, dryness, &c.: v.t. to ex-
pose to, or season by exposure to,
the air: sail to the windward of;
endure or resist bravely: v.i. to un-
dergo change by the action of the
weather.

7

(Above) Pages from *Tucson*.
(Opposite) Detail of
woman from *Tucson*; details
of doorway and label from
Cards of Houses.

"The creative mind plays with the objects it loves."
~ Carl Jung

storm (störm), n. a violent atmos-
pheric disturbance; tempest; heavy
fall of rain, snow, or hail; violent
commotion or agitation; tumult; calamity; violent assault on a fortified
place; v.t. to attack with violence or
open force; v.i. to blow violently;
be angry or rage.

8

Chapter 5

Places We
HAVE BEEN

Of course, an altered book scrapbook doesn't have to be about people at all. In *Tucson*, Karenann Young takes us on a tour of her hometown, complete with artifacts and the information savvy visitors need to know. Meanwhile, Gail Jacobson discards the notion of the scrapbook "album," turning her base book into a box filled with images of wonderful houses she has seen on her travels for *Cards of Houses*. By combining unusual techniques and common materials, these artists put an intriguing spin on the standard approach to the scrapbook.

From front cover to last page, Tucson reveals the geography, history, and culture of a city that blooms in the desert. Artist Karenann Young has combined maps, facts, and more to pay tribute to a place where golfers encounter rattlesnakes and Our Lady of Guadalupe appears at every turn. Karenann's choice of topics and imaginative presentation make this slim volume seem as comprehensive as the thickest guidebook.

(Opposite) Sun, a lizard, and a cactus—the sights of the desert set the mood, while an arch inspired by Southwestern architecture welcomes visitors to their personal tour of Tucson.

ARIZONA: GRAND CANYON STATE

STATE TREE: PALO VERDE

STATE BIRD: CACTUS WREN

STATE FISH: ARIZONA TROUT

STATE GEMSTONE: TURQUIOISE

CAPITOL OF ARIZONA: PHOENIX

ADMISSION TO STATEHOOD: FEB. 14, 1912

FLAG OF ARIZONA: RED AND YELLOW RAYS ARE SUNSHINE AND THE 13 COLONIES. THE COPPER STAR IS FOR THE COPPER MINING IN THE STATE.

Even though this is a desert, the land is full of plants all over the place!

Touches of acrylic paint give an ordinary photograph the brilliant color often found on postcards.

Plastic file tabs make pages easy to turn while reinforcing the guidebook theme.

Journaling becomes a graphic element when presented in carefully placed panels. Write your entire passage on scrap paper to plan your message and gauge how to place it within your layout.

Karenann honors the traditions and culture of the Southwest by incorporating the images associated with it, such as a skull from El Dia de los Muertos, a depiction of Our Lady of Guadalupe, and silver milagros (miracle) charms that the devout wear to express their faith.

Featured Technique

Pseudo-metal Background

With a combination of metallic tape, acrylic paint, and ballpoint pen, you can create a custom background for your layout. Learning this technique requires more patience than skill, yet even the most experienced artists can have fun with the effects it can produce.

Materials

— Acrylic paints: blue, purple

— Ballpoint pens: black, blue, purple

— Cardboard

— Charms

— Double-sided tape

— Metallic tapes: silver, copper

— Note

— Scissors

Instructions

1. Cover the page with silver metallic tape.

2. Adhere photograph in place, using double-sided tape.

3. Draw designs, using black, blue, and purple ballpoint pens.

4. Apply washes of acrylic paint.

5. Cut the cardboard to form a frame for the photograph. Cover the frame with copper tape.

6. Embellish with charms and note as desired.

"I look for new ways to use my materials. For instance, I may place images upside down, crop text for more interesting phrases, or combine dramatically dissimilar elements."

~ Karenann Young

103

For a complete scrapbook tour, be sure to include any area sights visitors simply have to see.

A Spanish-language background brings a little of Tucson's bilingual flavor to the tour.

To create a background page that blends with the sky of the photographs, Karenann applied blue paint to the map she had glued to her base book.

"Altered books can draw people past the surface details of life and give them something to think about by taking ordinary objects and images out of context. The perspective this gives us can help us see new possibilities in our lives. It's also a way to personalize our belongings the same way we personalize our homes.

"My first altered art projects involved cutting and rearranging black-and-white clipart images into new compositions. Over the years, I've learned through a lot of practice and from other artists and crafters. My preferred medium is paper with a dash of paint, chalk, pastels, colored pencils, and water-soluble crayons. I choose photos on instinct, going through my stash and pulling out whatever catches my eye at the time."

~ Karenann Young

Found objects in small plastic bags become educational artifacts when tagged and labeled like displays in a natural history museum. To create more room for three-dimensional elements such as these, remove a few pages between each spread.

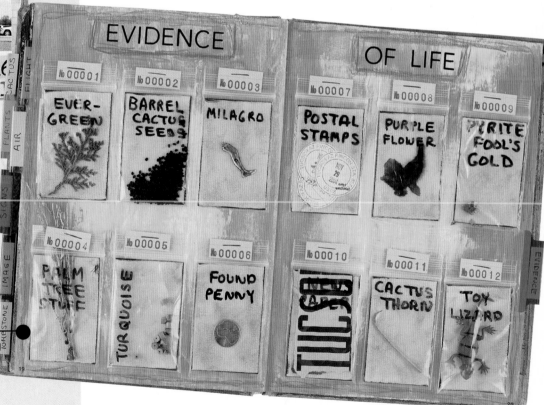

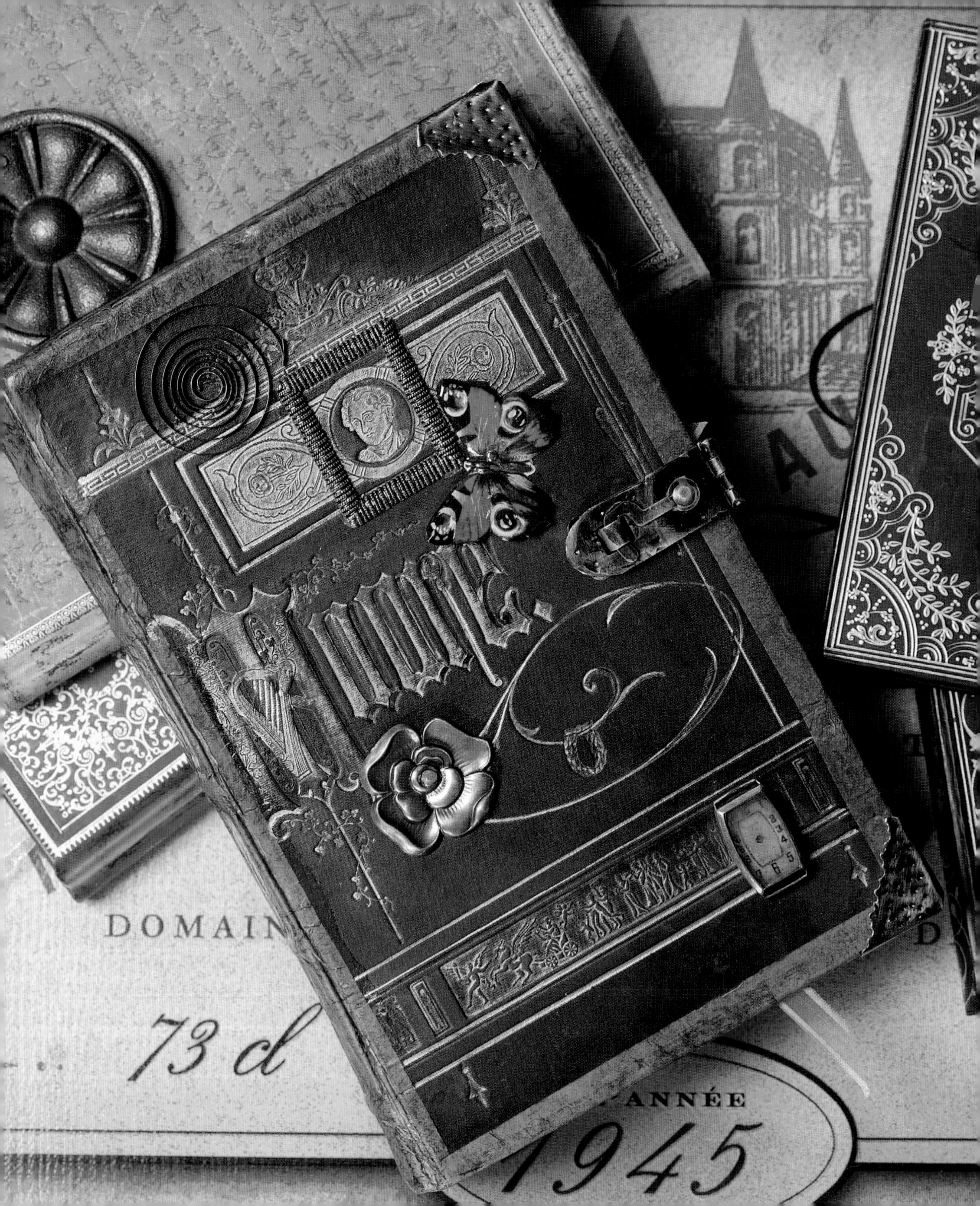
DOMAIN
73 d
ANNÉE
1945

Cards of Houses

Gail Jacobson

(Opposite) When Gail found this book, its spine was crumbling and the edges of the cover were frayed. To reinforce the damaged cover, she glued five short strings across the outside of the spine and added several layers of tissue paper. To finish, she rubbed brown and black shoe polish across the cover to achieve a rich patina. A touch-up with permanent gold pen brought the details of this cover back into shining relief.

Rather than build a house of cards, why not build cards of houses? In the nineteenth century, travelers bought inexpensive photographic prints mounted on cards to take home images of the places they toured. Called *cartes de visite*, these precursors to the picture postcard inspired Gail Jacobson to create *Cards of Houses*, a series of cards with images of Victorian architectural beauties stored between the covers of a book. By pushing the definition of the altered book scrapbook, Gail proves that the boundaries of this art form are only a matter of perception.

To make a sturdy container for a deck of cartes de visite, *paint a cigar box and adhere it to the inside of the back cover. Line the interior of the cover and cigar box with pages from a vintage calendar for a consistent style.*

> "It doesn't matter if you're icing a cake, painting a painting, knitting a sweater, or altering a book. It's all the same process."
> ~ Gail Jacobson

While most scrapbooks present relatively untouched photos on decorated pages, the designs for Cards of Houses began with Gail's treatment of photographs she had taken while visiting San Francisco and Boston.

Featured Technique

Victorian-style Postcard

Made of heavy paper and coated with clear spray paint, these cards are sturdy as well as beautiful, inviting viewers to shuffle through them and contemplate the places they depict.

Materials

— 24 lb. watercolor paper

— Brad

— Brushes for glue and paint

— Charms: key, number

— Clear glossy spray paint

— Craft knife

— Double-sided tape

— Embellishments: postage stamp, ticket

— Gold acrylic paint

— Mylar, 2" square

— Paste

— Photograph printed on photo transfer paper

— Spray bottle filled with water

Instructions

1. Measure and cut two identical rectangles of heavy watercolor paper. Set the second rectangle aside.

2. Print photograph onto photo transfer paper. Follow manufacturer's suggestions for printing and applying the image to the first rectangle of watercolor paper. *Note: Typically, some details will not transfer.*

3. Use a craft knife to cut a window in the first card. Apply a square of Mylar across the back of the window, using double-sided tape.

4. Set the first card face down on your work surface. Adhere a Mylar square over the window, using double-sided tape. Place the key charm on the Mylar.

5. Apply a coat of paste to the back of the first card. Place the second card onto the first. Use a heavy book to weigh them down until thoroughly dry.

6. Embellish with a postage stamp and an admission ticket.

7. Paint the edges of the card gold.

8. Finish with a coat of spray paint and attach the number charm, using a brad.

Centuries ago, "nostalgia" was the medical diagnosis for "homesickness." The soft, impressionistic images in Cards of Houses evoke the nostalgic mood that makes us yearn for places long ago and far away.

Cards of Houses

Gail Jacobson

"I grew up by the sea. My toys were shells, driftwood, and sea glass. Mom sewed our clothes, Dad built our house, and I learned that it's a pleasure to make your own things. Though I studied art in college, my real education came from my father's print shop where I spent many hours folding, gluing, and coloring paper scraps. Now, on any given day, the beds in my house may be unmade and dinner might be late, but the creative factory grinds on.

"I didn't understand altered books until I started making them myself. After all, why would you want a messed up book? But altered books are an amazing way to express creativity. Many of my ideas come to me in the twilight between waking and dreaming when ideas flow and unexpected connections appear. As a category, altered book scrapbooks inhabit this sort of in-between space."

~ Gail Jacobson

"The past is not a package one can lay away."
~ Emily Dickinson

(Above) Pages from *Florence*. (Opposite) Details of number and man with spectacles from *Honour the Past*; detail of woman from *Florence*.

Chapter 6

Honoring
THE PAST

Rescuing once-valued objects and styles from obscurity is what draws many to altered book scrapbooking. This art form invites us to revive vintage designs, as Lisa Cook does with images from the Forties and Fifties in *Florence*, a tribute to a woman's life. It also enables us to bring antique objects into the present, giving them new life through artistic interpretation, as we see in Nicole Landy's *Honour the Past*.

"In the search for our individual voices, the desire for acceptance fights the need to be unique. Therefore to be artists, we must take intense personal risk, embrace the thrill of creating, and let fear fall away."

~ *Lisa Cook*

When a friend saw Lisa Cook's altered book scrapbooks, she commissioned Lisa to create one for her mother Florence's birthday. Lisa worked with her friend to select a theme for each page and photos Lisa would copy and include in the scrapbook. The result: a lovely visual tribute to a beloved woman. The planning and care that were invested in this scrapbook shows on every page, making it a gift of inestimable value.

Vintage postcards are a motif throughout Florence. *Luckily, Lisa happened to have one that was not just the style and color she needed—it was also from Florence's hometown, Beaver, Wisconsin.*

Rectangles placed on a grid evoke the precision required for successful sailing maneuvers.

Dancing with her husband and sailing were two of Florence's favorite hobbies. Lisa brings them together in a single spread, using color to create unity and different layout styles for each activity.

Look for ways to describe an experience visually. For instance, circles placed in a curved line can mimic the sensation of spinning in a dance partner's arms.

Featured Technique

Quilted Book Bag

When giving an altered book scrapbook as a gift, make the presentation as sumptuous as the scrapbook itself. This quilted book bag is functional as well as pretty, as it protects the scrapbook's embellishments and tabs.

Materials

— Fabric-covered button

— Needle

— Quilted placemat

— Ribbon

— Sentiment tag

— Sewing machine

— Straight pins

— Thread

— Velvet leaves

Instructions

1. Lay the placemat on your work surface, pattern side down. Place the book in the center and fold up the bottom and sides. Pin in place.

2. Machine-stitch the bottom in place, mitering the corners. Stitch along the center to close the flaps, removing the pins as you proceed.

3. Add the button and embellishments by hand.

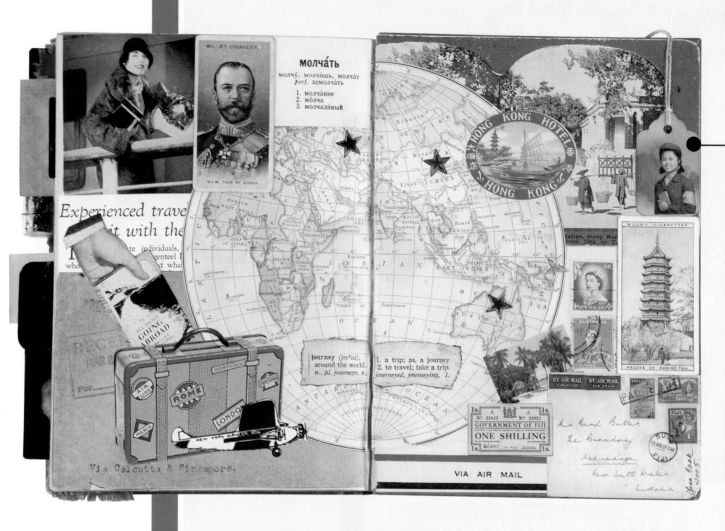

Since Florence was a schoolteacher and principal for many years, no retrospective of her life would be complete without at least one class photo. Stamped stars and party hats make the black-and-white image more festive.

In this layout, stars point out Australia, China, Russia, and Fiji on a map—places where Florence spent time as an exchange teacher.

"The bits and scraps we collect throughout our lives have the power to stir the soul with memory, yet most of us hide them away in a box or drawer. Altered book scrapbooking gives the artifacts from our lives a proper podium to tell their stories.

"I particularly enjoy using worn, old textbooks as a base for my art. I add copies of photographs and bits of ephemera to frame each chapter in someone's life. As a Home Economics teacher for more than twenty years, I often draw on the skills of my profession to add sewing, marbling, or hand-soldered charms to my creations. Making an altered book is much like building a puzzle: it demands that you think through each step of creation so that you can, in sewing terms, 'hide the seams' and present a finished piece that can be enjoyed for years to come."

~Lisa Cook

Stamped alphabet charts make a colorful background for a page celebrating a teacher's profession. The title, "Education of the Child," was torn from another book. A wash of walnut ink gives it an aged appearance to better match the image of a studying boy.

Featured Technique

Cloth Book Jacket

A cloth book jacket makes a lovely, yet durable, cover for your altered book scrapbook. For best results, select a thick fabric with a bit of give, like the plush upholstery sample used for *Honour the Past*.

Materials

— Embellishments

— Fabric

— Hot-glue gun and glue sticks

— Ruler

— Scissors

Honour the Past

Nicole Landy

Although the typical scrapbook revolves around people, places, and events known to its creator, artist Nicole Landy takes the altered book scrapbook on a voyage of pure imagination. She starts with vintage photos found at flea markets and creates stories about the people in them as she creates her layouts. For a scrapbook that invites contemplation, Nicole relies on graphical layouts and carefully chooses embellishments that fit each story she wants to tell. Nicole's inventive approach is a way to restore those forgotten by history to a place in human time.

Instructions

1. With book open, measure all sides, adding 3" extra to each side. Cut fabric to determined measurement.

2. Place fabric front side down on work surface. Fold down the top 3" of fabric and fold up the bottom 3" of fabric, forming a rectangle the height of the book. *Note: This will also create the pockets that hold the jacket to the book.*

3. Open the book and place it cover down on the fabric. Be sure that an even amount of fabric is visible on both sides.

4. Tuck the front cover into the left pocket.

5. Use hot glue to seal the top and bottom edge between the cover and the flap of the jacket.

6. Tuck the right side of the fabric over the back cover.

7. Repeat Step 5.

8. Adhere embellishments to the jacket, using hot glue.

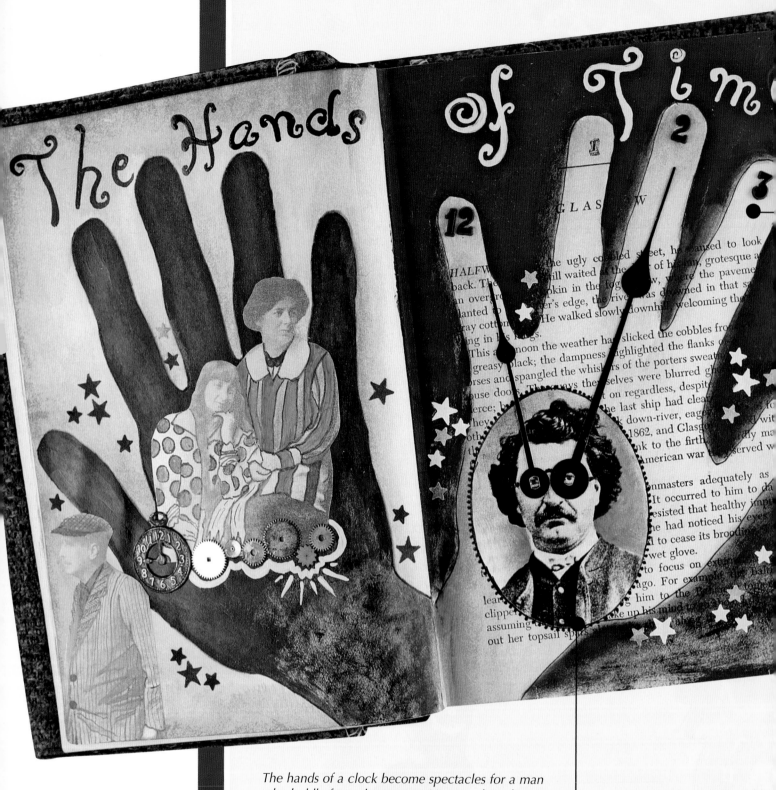

The hands of a clock become spectacles for a man who boldly faces the present. Heavy gel medium is good for securing metal elements such as these.

"Art may or may not put a roof over your head, but it's still a necessity of life. It addresses the spiritual side of existence, which is absolutely vital to a balanced human being." ~ Nicole Landy

Remember, any feature of the base book can become an element in your altered book scrapbook.

For Nicole, something about this woman's face indicates the wisdom, grace, and grit that deserve the title "Matriarch." A cold laminate transfer was used to apply the image to the page of text.

If you want to tell a story through images, pay special attention to details. To Nicole, a simple but sturdy key symbolizes the power of the matriarch.

Nicole Landy

"Altered art changes how you see the world. Once you realize that just about any object has the potential to become art, you stop taking things for granted. When I walk my dog, I look out for anything interesting I might find along the way. It's uncanny how what I do find relates directly to a piece I'm working on or thinking about, almost as if it was planted there expressly for me. It makes me feel connected to the world in a way that makes doing my solitary work anything but lonely.

"I particularly like rescuing old photographs. When I find an album at a flea market, I wonder how something that should be a family heirloom ever got lost like that. It's sad. I feel a connection with the past when I work with these old images; find their stories in my imagination and tell them the best I know how."

~Nicole Landy

To create handmade embellishments such as this key, cut shapes from 38-gauge metal foil, available at craft stores. Emboss with a blunt implement such as the handle of a paintbrush.

Meet the
ARTISTS

Madeline Arendt

Madeline is a freelance designer based in Illinois. Her clients include craft and floral supply manufacturers and her work appears regularly in craft-related magazines. Though her main focus has been on designing papercraft projects, clothes, and home fashions, she is always open to new possibilities.

Lisa Cook

Home Economics teacher Lisa Cook became a mixed-media artist when she celebrated turning fifty by creating fifty works of art. She creates altered books on commission and ornaments for shops in the Midwestern United States. Her art has been featured in *Somerset Studio*, *Legacy*, and *Transparent Art*.

Sarah Fishburn

Mixed-media collage artist Sarah Fishburn creates a range of objects from altered books to calendars and cards. Her work has appeared in numerous publications, including *Memory Makers*, *Legacy*, and *True Colors*. She also owns Rumphius Designs, a company located in Fort Collins, Colorado.

Lisa Hoffman

Designer and consultant Lisa Hoffman regularly teaches book arts and mixed-media art classes nationally. Her work has appeared in the Mary Lou Zeek Gallery in Salem, Oregon, the André Barnett Gallery in Baltimore, and publications including *True Colors*, and *Alphabetica*.

Gail Jacobson

Gail Jacobson's art has appeared in *Somerset Studio*, *Better Homes & Gardens*, and various galleries. She works with forms as diverse as pottery, abstract painting, needlecrafts, and Photoshop. She lives in rural Connecticut where she participates in an annual "Art at the Dump" festival, a show of work made exclusively from recycled materials.

Nicole Landy

Nicole Landy is a professional artist and mother of three who works and lives in Quebec. Her multi-dimensional pieces range from altered book scrapbooks and commemorative collage to fine art and can be seen in magazines such as *Somerset Studio* and *Artitude Zine*.

Shani Richart

North Carolina designer and photographer Shani Richart currently specializes in creating images of babies, mothers, and families. Her work has been described as sentimental, nostalgic, and inspirational. It can be seen in such publications as *Somerset Studio* and *Somerset Wedding*.

Susan Ure

Designer Susan Ure helps people find innovative ways to surround themselves with looks they love. A self-taught crafter, she has authored several books, including *Ten Minute Decorating*, *The Portable Crafter: Beading*, and *Scrapbooking Your Vacations*. Look for Susan in the instructional DVD, *Altered Scrapbooking for the First Time*.

Andrea Vetten-Marley

Andrea Vetten-Marley's scrapbook designs have been featured on television and in numerous publications, including *PaperKuts* and *Memory Makers* magazines. She has been a guest designer for HP Scrapbooking and is a member of the Timeless Touches design team.

Karenann Young

Karenann Young creates stand-alone collages, ceramics, miniatures, furniture, jewelry, and more. Her work has appeared in *Altered Books 101*, *Belle Armoire*, *RubberStampMadness*, and other publications; her designs grace numerous calendars, journals, and notecards.

Acknowledgements

Many thanks to Jo Packham. Without Jo's encouragement, I never would have risked authoring books. Jo is my hero and inspiration.

So many people make a book work. Jenn Gibbs used her clever writing skills to make my scribbles understandable. Thanks, Jenn.

Heather Harcourt's artistic eye made the pages flow. Zac's photography helped these projects look as beautiful as they really are. Thank you.

And last but never least, thank you to all the contributors whose work shows that there are many ways to make an altered book scrapbook.

Index

Credits

Editor:	Jennifer Gibbs
Book Designer:	Heather Harcourt
Photographer:	Zachary Williams
Graphic Illustrator:	Kim Coxey
Photo Stylist:	Andrea Hampton
Production Designer:	Ryan Christensen

inches to millimeters and centimeters							
inches	mm	cm	inches	cm	inches	cm
⅛	3	0.3	9	22.9	30	76.2
¼	6	0.6	10	25.4	31	78.7
½	13	1.3	12	30.5	33	83.8
⅝	16	1.6	13	33.0	34	86.4
¾	19	1.9	14	35.6	35	88.9
⅞	22	2.2	15	38.1	36	91.4
1	25	2.5	16	40.6	37	94.0
1¼	32	3.2	17	43.2	38	96.5
1½	38	3.8	18	45.7	39	99.1
1¾	44	4.4	19	48.3	40	101.6
2	51	5.1	20	50.8	41	104.1
2½	64	6.4	21	53.3	42	106.7
3	76	7.6	22	55.9	43	109.2
3½	89	8.9	23	58.4	44	111.8
4	102	10.2	24	61.0	45	114.3
4½	114	11.4	25	63.5	46	116.8
5	127	12.7	26	66.0	47	119.4
6	152	15.2	27	68.6	48	121.9
7	178	17.8	28	71.1	49	124.5
8	203	20.3	29	73.7	50	127.0